T0002524

I LOVE YOU A LATTE!

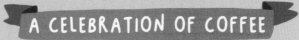

A CELEBRATION OF COFFEE

I LOVE YOU A LATTE!

A CELEBRATION OF COFFEE

MARINA OLIVEIRA

duopress

THANK YOU!

TO MY SON, LORENZO, WHO MAKES ME A BETTER PERSON EVERY DAY,

TO MY HUSBAND, FRED, FOR HIS UNCONDITIONAL SUPPORT,

TO MY FATHER, VALTER, WHO ALWAYS PUSHES ME TO DO BETTER,

AND TO MY MOM, RITA, WHO DRANK COUNTLESS CUPS OF COFFEE WITH

ME DURING THE MAKING OF THIS BOOK.

coffee

[káw-fee] noun.

a beverage essential to survival, made
from heaven-ground seeds that
can improve the drinker's mood
every morning

THE LEGEND OF THE ORIGIN OF
COFFEE

ONCE UPON A TIME IN 9TH-CENTURY ETHIOPIA, OR SO THEY SAY, THERE WAS A CURIOUS AND HUNGRY GOAT. HE LIVED WITH A GOATHERDER NAMED KALDI AND ROAMED THE COUNTRYSIDE MUNCHING ON GRASSES AND FRUITS TO HIS HEART'S CONTENT.

ONE DAY THE GOAT CAME ACROSS DELICIOUS COFFEE BERRIES. THEY TASTED SO GOOD! AFTER HE ATE THEM, THE GOAT BECAME SO ENERGETIC THAT HE STARTED DANCING.

KALDI COULDN'T BELIEVE HIS EYES. HE HAD TO TRY THIS FRUIT THAT HIS GOAT HAD DISCOVERED! HE SHARED THE BERRIES WITH AN ABBOT FRIEND AT A NEARBY MONASTERY.

THEY FIGURED OUT THAT THEY COULD BREW THE BERRIES INTO AN ENERGIZING BEVERAGE. SOON AFTER, COFFEE WAS INTRODUCED TO THE WORLD.

THE *little* ILLUSTRATED COFFEE *guide*

LET'S TAKE A LOOK AT TEN OF THE MOST POPULAR COFFEE DRINKS.

CONCENTRATED COFFEE ⌐

ESPRESSO

ESPRESSO IS VERY STRONG COFFEE THAT IS SERVED IN A SMALL CUP. ITS DARK-ROAST BEANS ARE VERY FINELY GROUND AND BREWED IN AN ESPRESSO MACHINE.

FOAMED MILK →

ESPRESSO →

← STEAMED MILK

CAFFÈ LATTE

A CAFFÈ LATTE IS MADE PRIMARILY FROM ESPRESSO AND STEAMED MILK. IT CONSISTS OF ONE-THIRD ESPRESSO, TWO-THIRDS STEAMED MILK, AND A LITTLE FOAM.

FOAMED MILK ↓

STEAMED MILK

← ESPRESSO

CAPPUCCINO

A CAPPUCCINO CONSISTS OF ONE-THIRD ESPRESSO, ONE-THIRD HEATED MILK, AND ONE-THIRD MILK FOAM.

STEAMED MILK ⌐

← ESPRESSO

CORTADO

A CORTADO IS AN ESPRESSO CUT WITH A SMALL AMOUNT OF WARM MILK TO REDUCE THE ACIDITY.

ESPRESSO →

← FOAMED OR STEAMED MILK

MACCHIATO

A MACCHIATO IS AN ESPRESSO THAT HAS BEEN TOPPED WITH A THIN LAYER OF FOAMED OR STEAMED MILK.

HOT WATER

ESPRESSO

AMERICANO

AN AMERICANO IS A MIX OF ONE PART ESPRESSO TO TWO PARTS HOT WATER.

SHORT ESPRESSO

RISTRETTO

THE MOST CONCENTRATED OF ALL ESPRESSOS, THE RISTRETTO ("RESTRICTED" IN ITALIAN) USES LESS HOT WATER FOR A RICHER FLAVOR.

MILK

ESPRESSO

CAFÉ AU LAIT

"CAFÉ AU LAIT" IS FRENCH FOR "COFFEE WITH MILK." THE DRINK ORIGINATED IN FRANCE AND IS MADE WITH DRIP COFFEE AND STEAMED MILK.

FOAM

STEAMED MILK

ESPRESSO

FLAT WHITE

A FLAT WHITE CONSISTS OF ONE-THIRD ESPRESSO, TWO-THIRDS STEAMED MILK, AND A LITTLE FOAM.

WHIPPED CREAM

STEAMED MILK

CHOCOLATE

ESPRESSO

MOCHA

A MOCHA IS TYPICALLY ONE-THIRD ESPRESSO, TWO-THIRDS STEAMED MILK, WHIPPED CREAM, AND CHOCOLATE SYRUP.

7

WHERE HAVE YOU BEAN My whole LIFE?

COFFEE : FROM SEED TO CUP

1 PLANTING

There are two main species of coffee plants, arabica and robusta.

4. MILLING

During this step any fruit surrounding the beans will be removed.

2. PICKING

Generally 4-5 years after being planted, coffee cherries are ready to harvest.

3 PROCESSING

Coffee cherries can be processed in many ways, but two of the most common are:

DRY PROCESSING

An older method. Beans are dried naturally in the sun.

5. ROASTING

The young beans are roasted at high temperatures. The duration and temperature of the roast will result in different flavors.

6. PACKAGING

The beans need to be protected from air and moisture.

7. GRINDING

The freshness, size, and quality of grind have a big effect on how the coffee will taste.

8. BREWING

There are many ways to brew a cup of coffee. Each method of brewing coffee can impact the final flavor.

PROCESSING METHOD AFFECTS THE QUALITY OF THE END RESULT.

WET PROCESSING

This method uses lots of water and equipment.

9. DRINKING

There's a long way from seed to cup, yet every step makes your coffee more special.

COFFEE IS FOR PLANT LOVERS

Plants and coffee are the perfect pair — after all, the coffee bean originates from a plant! A woody evergreen, the coffee plant grows to look much like a tree, with a vertical trunk. Its sweet flowers become fruits (like a cherry) after they are pollinated. The bean is housed inside the cherry fruit, like a pit.

"BEHIND EVERY SUCCESSFUL WOMAN IS A SUBSTANTIAL AMOUNT OF COFFEE"

– Stephanie Piro

MY LIFE in A PIE CHART

the **ANTIQUE**

the **ROMANTIC**

the **ARTISTIC**

WHAT COFFEE MUG ARE YOU?

the **BASIC**

the **MINIMALIST**

the **CHARMING**

the
FUNNY

the
MODERN

the
TRENDY

the
CLASSIC

the
CAMPER

the
RETRO

the
ON THE GO

COFFEE
ON THE GO

FROSTY CARAMEL CAPPUCCINO

Too hot outside for your favorite cappuccino? Try this cold caramel-flavored version topped with whipped cream

MAKES 2 SERVINGS

INGREDIENTS

1 CUP HALF AND HALF

2 TEASPOONS INSTANT COFFEE OR ESPRESSO POWDER

1 CUP WHOLE MILK

3 TABLESPOONS PLUS 2 TEASPOONS DULCE DE LECHE OR CARAMEL SYRUP

4 TABLESPOONS WHIPPED CREAM

8 TO 10 ICE CUBES

DIRECTIONS

1. PLACE THE HALF AND HALF, MILK, INSTANT COFFEE, 3 TABLESPOONS DULCE DE LECHE, AND ICE CUBES IN A BLENDER. PROCESS UNTIL SMOOTH.

2. POUR THE FROZEN CAPPUCCINO INTO CHILLED OR DOUBLE-WALLED GLASSES. TOP WITH WHIPPED CREAM AND DRIZZLE WITH THE REMAINING DULCE DE LECHE. SERVE IMMEDIATELY.

ENJOY!

BUT FIRST, COFFEE

sugar

But
Second,
Coffee

Food Water

23

CHOCOLATE

COOKIE

DONUT

10 BEST
SNACKS
TO HAVE WITH COFFEE

MUFFIN

MACARON

BROWNIE

CROISSANT

WAFFLES

BACON, EGG, and CHEESE

STRAWBERRY CHEESECAKE

ALFAJOR

CINNAMON ROLL

BENEFITS OF DRINKING COFFEE

Coffee is the morning ritual for many people in the world. It fuels you with energy and helps kick-start the day. Coffee may have several health benefits when consumed in moderation.

IMPROVES ENERGY levels

ENHANCES MENTAL Performance

Boosts YOUR METABOLIC RATE

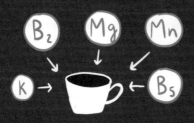

CONTAINS *Essential* NUTRIENTS

MAY LOWER RISKS OF SEVERAL CONDITIONS & DISEASES

MORE LIKELY TO LIVE LONGER

HELPS PROMOTE *healthy skin* WITH ANTIOXIDANTS

ELEVATES & MOOD PREVENTS DEPRESSION

"IF IT WEREN'T FOR THE COFFEE, I'D HAVE NO IDENTIFIABLE PERSONALITY WHATSOEVER"
— DAVID LETTERMAN

28

HOW DO YOU TAKE YOUR COFFEE?

CAFETONE 11-060
Milk

CAFETONE 14-1119
Still Not Coffee

CAFETONE 16-1439
A Little Caffeine

CAFETONE 16-1429
Cardboard

CAFETONE 16-1432
Tawny

CAFETONE 18-0950
Just a Splash

CAFETONE 19-1218
Ran Out of Milk

CAFETONE 19-4305
Rough Night

BREW AND BOOKS

Nothing goes with coffee quite like a book, as any visitors to these famous literary cafes can attest:

ANTICO CAFFÈ GRECO, ROME

Watering hole of many historic figures, including Franz Liszt, James Joyce, Friedrich Nietzsche, John Keats, Johann Wolfgang von Goethe, and Hans Christian Andersen.

CAFÉ LA ROTONDE, PARIS

Noted in The Sun Also Rises by Ernest Hemingway, one of many ex-pat patrons along with T.S. Eliot, F. Scott Fitzgerald, and Gertrude Stein.

VESUVIO CAFÉ, SAN FRANCISCO

Home to artists and poets of the Beat Generation, including Jack Kerouac, Dylan Thomas, and Allen Ginsberg.

The moka pot brews espresso on the stovetop, using boiling water and steam to brew ground coffee.

MOKA ESPRESSO POT

The AeroPress brews a single serving of coffee through a filter. Pressing down on a plunger forces water through the grounds.

AEROPRESS

THE LITTLE *illustrated* **COFFEE MAKER & ACCESSORY · GUIDE ·**

ESPRESSO

An espresso machine pumps pressurized water through a puck of ground espresso beans at a specific temperature.

FRENCH PRESS

Ground coffee and hot water mingle together in the cylindrical pot of a French press. A filter is "pressed" down with a plunger to trap the grounds at the bottom.

IBRIK

An ibrik is a Turkish coffee pot that steeps very finely ground beans over a low flame.

CHEMEX

A carafe for pour-over brewing, a Chemex holds grounds in a cone-shaped filter and collects coffee in the base.

HARIO V60

Produced in Japan, the V60 is a dripper that comes in glass, ceramic, or plastic for pour-over coffee. It uses a paper filter and sits directly on your coffee cup.

GOOSENECK KETTLE

With its thin, precise spout, the gooseneck kettle was designed especially for pour-over coffee preparation.

MANUAL GRINDER

Manual grinders use a hand crank to send beans through two burrs that create a consistent grind.

SIPHON

The siphon is an elaborate dual-chamber setup that uses water vapor to create a vacuum that brews coffee.

THE 10 TYPES OF
COFFEE DRINKERS
WHICH ONE ARE YOU?

The ESPRESSO
Enthusiast

The LATTE
Lover

The MOCHA
Aficionado

The CAPPUCCINO
Connoisseur

The COLD BREW
Appreciator

The **INSTANT** COFFEE
Admirer

The **FANCY**
Orderer

The **DECAF**
Devotee

The **FRAPPE**
Fanatic

The **POUR OVER**
Brewer

Lavender and Honey
Iced Coffee

Ingredients

YIELDS 1 BEVERAGE

ICE, AS DESIRED

2 TABLESPOONS LAVENDER HONEY SYRUP (RECIPE FOLLOWS)

1/3 CUP COFFEE CONCENTRATE SUCH AS GRADY'S OR CHAMELEON

1/3 CUP WHOLE MILK

DIRECTIONS

1   FILL a GLASS OR MUG WITH ICE, aS DESIRED.

2   PLACE THE LAVENDER HONEY SYRUP

    IN a GLASS MEASURING CUP.

3   ADD THE COFFEE CONCENTRATE aND MILK

    TO THE SYRUP aND WHISK TO COMBINE .
    POUR THE MIXTURE OVER ICE aND ENJOY!

LAVENDER HONEY SYRUP

2 TEASPOONS DRIED LAVENDER BUDS
1/2 CUP SUGAR
1/2 CUP WATER
1/2 CUP HONEY

1. COMBINE THE DRIED LAVENDER, SUGAR,
WATER, AND HONEY IN A SMALL SAUCEPAN
OVER MEDIUM HEAT. STIR UNTIL THE
SUGAR DISSOLVES, ABOUT 5 MINUTES.
2. TAKE THE PAN OFF THE HEAT TO
COOL COMPLETELY. STRAIN OUT THE
DRIED LAVENDER.

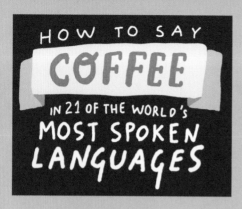

HOW TO SAY COFFEE
IN 21 OF THE WORLD'S MOST SPOKEN LANGUAGES

Кофе

Café

FRENCH, SPANISH, PORTUGUESE

RUSSIAN

ITALIAN

Caffè

KOFFIE ROBUST

KAHVE ROASTED

TURKISH

HINDI

PREMIUM
कॉफ़ी BLEND

AFRIKAANS & DUTCH

咖啡
GROUND COFFEE

CHINESE

38

GERMAN

FINNISH

JAPANESE

ENGLISH

KOREAN

ROMANIAN

SWEDISH

CROATIAN & SLOVENIAN

MALAY & INDONESIAN

"I HAVE MEASURED OUT MY LIFE WITH COFFEE SPOONS"
—T.S. Eliot

A FEW THINGS ABOUT
COFFEE

1 COFFEE is one of the most popular drinks in the world.

2 FINLAND is the country that consumes the most coffee in the world.

3 BRAZIL produces 40% of the world's coffee, more than any other country.

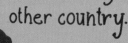

4 It takes a day to fully eliminate caffeine from your system.

5 People from NEW YORK drink seven times more coffee than people in other cities in the United States.

6 Coffee is most EFFECTIVE if you drink it between 9:30 AM and 11:30 AM.

7 Humans consume about **2.25** billon cups of coffee every day.

8 The most expensive coffee in the world is BLACK IVORY COFFEE.

It's produced from partly digested coffee cherries, eaten and defecated by Thai elephants.

HOW TO BREW YOUR COFFEE

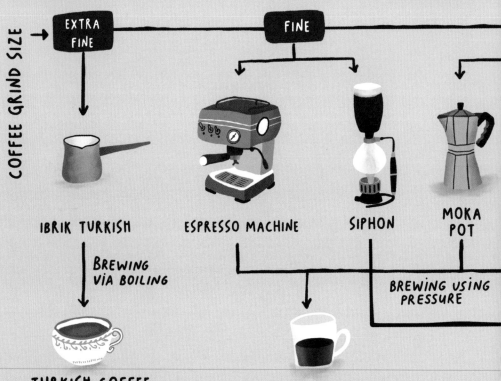

COFFEE GRIND SIZE →

EXTRA FINE

FINE

IBRIK TURKISH

ESPRESSO MACHINE

SIPHON

MOKA POT

BREWING VIA BOILING

BREWING USING PRESSURE

TURKISH COFFEE

ESPRESSO

Coffee is personal - you probably already have a favorite way to brew. Even so maybe you'd like to shake things up and try a new method.

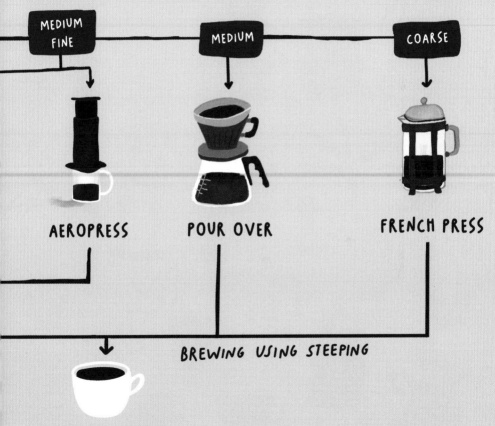

MEDIUM FINE

MEDIUM

COARSE

AEROPRESS

POUR OVER

FRENCH PRESS

BREWING USING STEEPING

CUP OF COFFEE

Everything's going to *bean* all right !

FUELING YOUR BICYCLE ENGINE

The French bicycle-themed coffeehouse Le Vélocipède has been around since 1882, when it was the headquarters of the Parisian bicycle club.

CARAMEL BROWNIE

COFFEE

THE PERFECT WINTER WARMER

Makes 1 Mug

INGREDIENTS

1 cup freshly brewed coffee
2 tablespoons milk chocolate chips
1 tablespoon French vanilla creamer
Whipped cream, as desired
1 brownie
Caramel sauce or dulce de leche, to taste

INSTRUCTIONS

1. Pour the coffee into a mug, sprinkle in the chocolate chips, and stir to melt them.

2. Add the French vanilla creamer and stir to combine.

3. Top with whipped cream, as desired. Crumble the brownie on top and drizzle with caramel sauce.

WHAT IS CASCARA?

AFTER THE COFFEE BEAN HAS BEEN REMOVED FROM THE FRUIT OF THE COFFEE CHERRY, THE FRUIT IS DRIED. THOSE DRIED SKINS ARE CALLED CASCARA, AND THEY CAN BE USED TO CREATE A DRINK SIMILAR TO TEA.

← BEAN

CHERRY ←

CASCARA SMELLS LIKE CHOCOLATE-COVERED CHERRIES

IN SOME COUNTRIES, ESPECIALLY BOLIVIA AND YEMEN, THIS CHERRY IS BREWED AS A TEA.

TO MAKE THE TEA:

Boil water until it reaches 200 F.
Steep 20 grams of cascara in
400 grams of water for 4 minutes
(or keep infusing up to 12 minutes if
you prefer a stronger flavor). Drain
the tea and discard the pulp.

TOP 6
COFFEE SHOPS
on a TV Series

MONK'S CAFE

JERRY, ELAINE, GEORGE, AND KRAMER SPEND LOTS OF TIME AT THIS FICTIONAL COFFEE SHOP. A REAL DINER WAS USED FOR THE EXTERIOR SCENES – TOM'S RESTAURANT, ON BROADWAY AND 112TH STREET IN MANHATTAN.

Seinfeld

CENTRAL PERK

F·R·I·E·N·D·S

PERHAPS ONE OF THE MOST FAMOUS FICTIONAL COFFEE SHOPS, CENTRAL PERK, AND ITS LARGE ORANGE COUCH, WAS THE HUB OF ACTIVITY DURING ALL TEN OF THE SHOW'S SEASONS.

FROM THE PILOT EPISODE OF *GILMORE GIRLS*, LUKE'S DINER IS AN IMPORTANT PLACE FOR LORELAI (AND RORY) GILMORE TO GET THEIR CAFFEINE FIXES.

Luke's
Gilmore girls

BEVERLY 90210 HILLS

THE FICTIONAL RETRO DINER IN THE BEVERLY HILLS DRAMA *90210* WAS KNOWN AS THE PEACH PIT. LIKE ANY GOOD DINER, IT SERVED COFFEE BUT WAS KNOWN FOR ITS MEGA BURGER.

PEACH PIT

BEVERLY HILLS, CA 90210

felicity

NO, IT'S NOT A FANCY NEW YORK GROCERY STORE – IT'S A FICTIONAL COFFEE SHOP WHERE MAIN CHARACTER FELICITY WORKS DURING COLLEGE. THE WB COPIED THE GROCER'S NAME, WHICH MADE PLENTY OF PEOPLE VISITING THE REAL-LIFE DEAN & DELUCA CONFUSED.

DEAN & DELUCA

Café Nervosa

SEATTLE IS THE COFFEE CAPITAL OF THE U.S., SO ANY SITCOM SET THERE MUST HAVE A COFFEE SHOP!

FRASIER

DON'T TALK
TO ME UNTIL
I'VE HAD MY
COFFEE

"EVEN BAD COFFEE *is Better* THAN NO *Coffee* AT ALL"

—DAVID LYNCH

Honey *spiced* Latte

A nice balance between sweet and spicy
with a soothing finish.

INGREDIENTS

1 1/3 cups whole milk

2 tablespoons honey

2 tablespoons molasses

4 teaspoons sugar

1/8 teaspoon ground cloves

1/4 teaspoon ground ginger

1/4 teaspoon ground cinnamon

1/4 teaspoon ground cardamom

1/8 teaspoon ground nutmeg

1 1/2 cups freshly brewed coffee

Whipped cream if desired

INSTRUCTIONS

1. Place the milk, honey, molasses, sugar, and spices in a small saucepan over medium heat. Stir until the sugar is dissolved and the mixture is steaming, about 5 minutes.

2. Transfer the milk-honey mixture to a blender and process until foamy, 15 seconds.

3. Pour the foamy mixture into 4 mugs. Add the coffee to each one to fill the mug. Garnish with whipped cream, as desired.

Makes 4 Lattes

BECAUSE YOU NEED YOUR
COFFEE ON THE GO

Mobile coffee has been an essential part of city living in the U.S. ever since street vendors began selling food and drink from pushcarts in 1700s' New Amsterdam (now NYC).

I have
coffeelings for you !

A DAY IN THE LIFE:
BARISTA

In Spanish and Italian, "barista" means "bartender" and refers to someone who prepares any kind of drink behind a counter. In English, it refers specifically to coffee "artists."

66

TOOLS OF A BARISTA

THERMOMETER

Helps you steam the milk to the perfect temperature

FILTER BASKET

Crucial for quality control and consistent extraction

TAMPER

Used to pack grounds into the basket of an espresso machine

SCALE

Measuring your coffee and water gives you complete control over the volume

GRINDER

Grinding beans to a uniform size makes for a consistent cup

THINGS TO DO WITH LEFTOVER COFFEE

USE IT TO STAIN RAW FURNITURE
Coffee makes a natural alternative to store-bought wood stains.

WASH YOUR **HAIR** WITH IT TO LEAVE YOUR HAIR NOT ONLY SOFT AND SMOOTH BUT HEALTHY AND STRONG.

FREEZE COFFEE IN ICE-CUBE TRAYS FOR THE NEXT TIME YOU ARE CRAVING AN ICED COFFEE.

BAKE BROWNIES

Adding coffee to brownies will enhance the chocolate flavor.

USE IT AS FERTILIZER IN YOUR GARDEN.

Simply sprinkle coffee grounds onto the soil surrounding your plants.

Make an **EXFOLIATING** coffee scrub out of leftover grounds, melted coconut oil, brown sugar, and vanilla extract.

HOT *Ginger* COFFEE

The perfect coffee drink to sip next to the fireplace

MAKES 6 BEVERAGES

INGREDIENTS

6 heaping tablespoons
COFFEE GROUNDS

1 tablespoon
ORANGE ZEST,
plus more for garnish

1 tablespoon chopped
crystallized **GINGER,**
plus more for garnish

1/2 teaspoon
**GROUND
CINNAMON**

6 cups
COLD WATER

WHIPPED CREAM
as desired

INSTRUCTIONS

1. Combine the coffee grounds, orange zest, ginger, and cinnamon in the filter of a drip coffee maker. Brew with the cold water.

2. Pour the ginger coffee into mugs. Garnish with whipped cream, orange zest, and crystallized ginger, as desired.

71

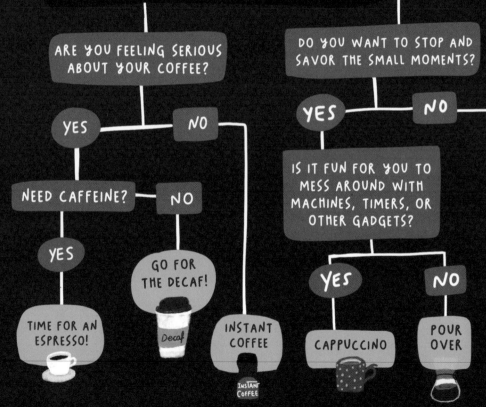

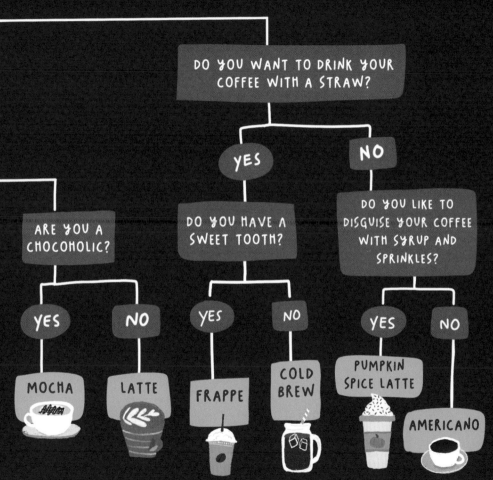

DO YOU WANT TO DRINK YOUR COFFEE WITH A STRAW?

YES

NO

ARE YOU A CHOCOHOLIC?

DO YOU HAVE A SWEET TOOTH?

DO YOU LIKE TO DISGUISE YOUR COFFEE WITH SYRUP AND SPRINKLES?

YES

NO

YES

NO

YES

NO

MOCHA

LATTE

FRAPPE

COLD BREW

PUMPKIN SPICE LATTE

AMERICANO

MEXICAN SPICED
MOCHA

Coffee with cinnamon and chili powder: The
perfect kick to help you wake up.

MAKES 1 SERVING

INGREDIENTS

2 TABLESPOONS POWDERED SUGAR

1 TABLESPOON COCOA POWDER

1/4 TEASPOON GROUND CINNAMON

1/4 CUP WHOLE MILK

1/8 TEASPOON CHILI POWDER

1 CUP FRESHLY BREWED COFFEE

WHIPPED CREAM AS DESIRED

INSTRUCTIONS

1. PLACE THE POWDERED SUGAR, COCOA POWDER, CINNAMON, AND CHILI POWDER IN A COFFEE MUG. STIR TO COMBINE.

2. POUR IN THE COFFEE, STIRRING UNTIL THE SUGAR AND SPICES ARE DISSOLVED. STIR IN THE MILK.

3. TOP WITH WHIPPED CREAM AND DUST WITH CINNAMON, AS DESIRED.

COFFEE
TASTES BETTER when
WE'RE TOGETHER

TOP 8 REASONS TO GO TO A COFFEE SHOP

1

A LONG-OVERDUE MEETING WITH A FRIEND

2

YOU'RE HUNGRY, YOU NEED FUEL, AND ONLY A FLAKY PASTRY OR CRUMBLY MUFFIN WITH ESPRESSO WILL DO

3 FOR THE PEOPLE WATCHING

4

THE BARISTA IS CUTE

5

YOU'RE WRITING THE NEXT
GREAT BEST-SELLING NOVEL

6

YOU WANT TO GET TO KNOW YOUR
NEW WORK COLLEAGUE BETTER

7

YOU CAN'T MAKE
ESPRESSO DRINKS
AT HOME THAT ARE
QUITE AS DELICIOUS

8

YOU FEEL MORE
CREATIVE

CELEBRATE COFFEE DAY!

International Coffee Day (October 1st) is the day to enjoy and appreciate your beverage, and maybe even pick one up for free or at a discounted price at some stores.

you are
BREWTIFUL

HOT ORANGE COFFEE

2 TABLESPOONS SUGAR

3 TEASPOONS INSTANT COFFEE POWDER

1 TEASPOON ORANGE ZEST

1 TABLESPOON WARM WATER

3 CUPS WHOLE MILK

1. PLACE THE GROUND COFFEE, SUGAR, AND WATER IN A BOWL AND WHISK TO COMBINE.

2. PLACE THE MILK AND ORANGE ZEST IN A SAUCEPAN OVER MEDIUM HEAT UNTIL IT COMES TO A BOIL. REDUCE THE HEAT AND SIMMER FOR 2 MINUTES.

3. ADD THE MILK TO THE COFFEE AND STIR WELL. SERVE HOT.

ENJOY!

MAKE 2 LARGE MUGS

COFFEE Grinders

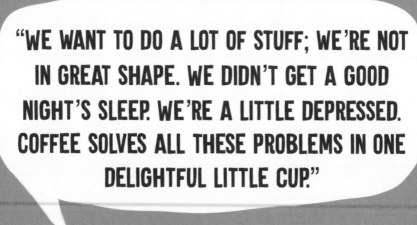

"WE WANT TO DO A LOT OF STUFF; WE'RE NOT IN GREAT SHAPE. WE DIDN'T GET A GOOD NIGHT'S SLEEP. WE'RE A LITTLE DEPRESSED. COFFEE SOLVES ALL THESE PROBLEMS IN ONE DELIGHTFUL LITTLE CUP."

– JERRY SEINFELD

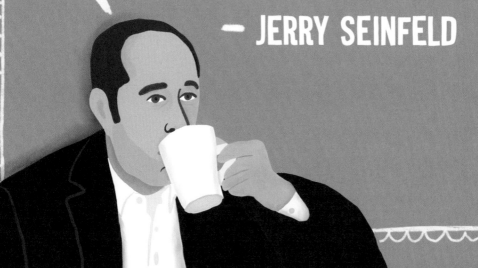

COMMON COFFEE TERMS TO KNOW

AFFOGATO

Meaning "drowned" in Italian, an espresso poured over vanilla ice cream.

CAFFEINE

The bitter, stimulating compound C8H10N4O2.

ARABICA

A species of coffee plant that produces high-quality beans with a softer, sweeter taste than Robusta. Only found in the wild in the forests of Ethiopia.

DOPPIO

A double espresso.

CREMA

Thick, caramel-colored foam that covers the surface of an espresso.

REDEYE

A double-whammy: drip coffee with an espresso shot.

BLOOM

When coffee grounds meet water, a quick, bubbling reaction happens and sour carbon dioxide is released.

DARK ROAST

Coffee beans roasted to a medium-dark color. Coffee oils appear on the surface of the beans and varietal flavors are muted.

ROBUSTA

A high-yield variety of coffee plant that is more bitter, but more caffeinated, than arabica, and more tolerant of warmer climates.

DALGONA*
coffee

* This name is credited to South Korean actor Jung Il-woo; the drink, or a close relative, is also known as a frappe

MAKES 1 SERVING

YOU WILL NEED:

2 TABLESPOONS SUGAR

1 CUP WHOLE MILK

1 CUP ICE

2 TABLESPOONS INSTANT COFFEE

2 TABLESPOONS HOT WATER

PLACE THE INSTANT COFFEE, SUGAR, AND HOT WATER IN A MEDIUM MIXING BOWL.

USE AN ELECTRIC MIXER OR A WHISK TO WHIP THE MIXTURE UNTIL IT IS LIGHT BROWN, FLUFFY, CREAMY, AND WILL HOLD SOFT PEAKS.

FILL A GLASS WITH ICE AND THEN MILK UNTIL IT IS THREE-QUARTERS FULL, THEN DOLLOP AND SWIRL THE WHIPPED COFFEE ON TOP.

BEANS on SCREEN

"IT'S ALL IN THE GRIND, SIZEMORE. CAN'T BE TOO FINE, CAN'T BE TOO COARSE. THIS, MY FRIEND, IS A SCIENCE."
EWAN MCGREGOR - BLACK HAWK DOWN

"GET ME SOME COFFEE. HALF AND HALF. THREE SWEET'N LOWS. IN A REAL CUP. NOT ONE OF THOSE PAPER OR STYROFOAM THINGS."
MORGAN FREEMAN - OLYMPUS HAS FALLEN

POPCORN

94

"CONGRATULATIONS! WORLD'S BEST
CUP OF COFFEE! GREAT JOB, EVERYBODY!
IT'S GREAT TO BE HERE."

WILL FERRELL - <u>ELF</u>

HOLLYWOOD

"IS THERE SOME REASON THAT MY
COFFEE ISN'T HERE? HAS SHE DIED
OR SOMETHING?"

MERYL STREEP - <u>THE DEVIL WEARS PRADA</u>

"I CAN'T FACE THE WORLD IN
THE MORNING. I MUST HAVE COFFEE
BEFORE I CAN SPEAK."

JOSEPH COTTEN - <u>SHADOW OF A DOUBT</u>

The End

95

" What on earth could be more luxurious than a sofa, a book, and a cup of coffee ? "

— ANTHONY TROLLOPE

97

WELCOME TO COFFEE Town

ark Street
OFFEE
OVE

ELEVATOR AT
ATTE STREET

STORE

LAVENDER LATTE

MAKES 1 BEVERAGE

FOR THE LAVENDER SYRUP:

1/4 CUP SUGAR

1/4 CUP WATER

1 TABLESPOON DRIED LAVENDER BUDS

1. COMBINE THE DRIED LAVENDER, SUGAR, AND WATER IN A SMALL SAUCEPAN OVER MEDIUM HEAT. STIR UNTIL THE SUGAR DISSOLVES, ABOUT 5 MINUTES.

2. TAKE THE PAN OFF THE HEAT TO COOL COMPLETELY. STRAIN OUT THE DRIED LAVENDER.

FOR THE LATTE:

1 TABLESPOON LAVENDER SYRUP

FRESHLY BREWED HOT COFFEE

STEAMED AND FROTHED OAT MILK

INSTRUCTIONS

1. PLACE THE LAVENDER SYRUP IN A COFFEE CUP AND POUR IN AS MUCH COFFEE AS DESIRED. STIR TO COMBINE.

2. TOP WITH FROTHY OAT MILK AS DESIRED.

"COFFEE FIRST.
SCHEMES
Later."

— LEANNA RENEE HIEBER
DARKER STILL

103

COFFEEHOUSE REGULAR

J.S. Bach

Coffee arrived in Europe around the same time that Johann Sebastian Bach was born. It quickly became a popular beverage. Bach himself regularly performed at Cafe Zimmerman (Zimmermannsches Kaffeehaus) in Leipzig, Germany. His secular and comedic cantata (or "mini-opera") about a caffeine-obsessed young woman named Lieschen uses text written by Picander, aka Christian Friedrich Henrici.

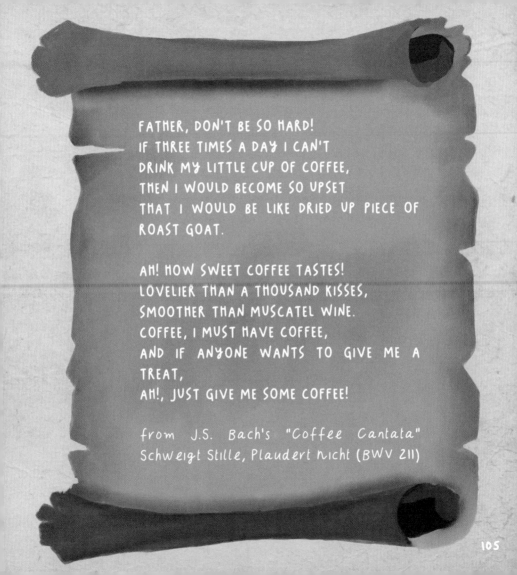

FATHER, DON'T BE SO HARD!
IF THREE TIMES A DAY I CAN'T
DRINK MY LITTLE CUP OF COFFEE,
THEN I WOULD BECOME SO UPSET
THAT I WOULD BE LIKE DRIED UP PIECE OF
ROAST GOAT.

AH! HOW SWEET COFFEE TASTES!
LOVELIER THAN A THOUSAND KISSES,
SMOOTHER THAN MUSCATEL WINE.
COFFEE, I MUST HAVE COFFEE,
AND IF ANYONE WANTS TO GIVE ME A
TREAT,
AH!, JUST GIVE ME SOME COFFEE!

from J.S. Bach's "Coffee Cantata"
Schweigt Stille, Plaudert Nicht (BWV 211)

WINTER

SPRING

106

The history of the
COFFEE MACHINE

15th CENTURY	AROUND 1800	1822	1830

TURKISH COFFEE MAKER

PERCOLATOR

ESPRESSO MACHINE

VACCUM COFFEE MAKER

It is in the 15th century in the Near East that the first coffee makers appear. A simple design, ground coffee is mixed with water over fire and left to boil.

The first design for a percolator, or a machine that cycles water through coffee grounds, improves the taste of coffee thanks to Archbishop of Paris Jean-Baptiste de Belloy.

Frenchman Louis-Bernard Rabaut debuts a machine that forces water through finely ground coffee beans – an early espresso maker!

The first patent for a siphon, or vacuum coffee maker, is registered by a German known as S. Loeff. A decade later, Mme. Vassieux of Lyons, France, popularizes the model of design and function that we know today.

1908	1929	1933	1972

DRIP COFFEE MAKER

FRENCH PRESS

ITALIAN COFFEE MAKER

AUTOMATIC DRIP COFFEE MACHINE

German housewife Melitta Bentz creates the first manual filter coffee maker.

Surprisingly, an Italian designer, Attilio Calimani, invents the modern version of the French press. However, two Frenchmen, Henri-Otto Mayer and Jacques-Victor Delforge, had patented a similar infusion brewer design in 1852.

Italian engineer Alfonso Bialetti creates and gives his name to the famous brand Moka Express, named for the city of Mocha, Yemen.

Vincent Marotta's invention, Mr. Coffee, signals the end of the percolator and revolutionizes home coffee making.

"AS LONG AS THERE WAS COFFEE IN THE WORLD, HOW BAD COULD THINGS BE?"

— CASSANDRA CLARE
CITY OF ASHES

A NOT-SO-COMPREHENSIVE LIST OF ENORMOUS COFFEE POTS

BOB'S JAVA JIVE
TACOMA, WA

Built in 1927, this large coffee pot-shaped building became a cultural landmark.

KOONTZ COFFEE POT
BEDFORD, PA

Made of bricks and sheet metal, this large pot has been a diner, bus station, and bar.

SWEDISH COFFEE POT TOWER
KINGSBURG, CA

In Kingsburg, a Swedish "village," a giant coffee pot serves as the water tower.

THE WORLD'S LARGEST COFFEE POT
SASKATCHEWAN, CANADA

Standing 24 ft. tall, this coffee pot would hold 150,000 cups if filled with coffee.

THE DALLAH COFFEE POT
DOHA, QATAR

A symbol of hospitality, a dallah is considered a welcoming gesture in the Arabic world.

COFFEE POT ART

THE COFFEE POT
LEXINGTON, VA

The spout of this coffee pot can release steam, as part of its realistic appeal.

MORE
ESPRESSO
LESS
DEPRESSO

ABOUT THE AUTHOR

MARINA OLIVEIRA IS THE ILLUSTRATOR BEHIND COTTONFLOWER STUDIO.
SHE STUDIED ARCHITECTURE AT NORTHEASTERN UNIVERSITY IN BOSTON
AND HAS WORKED AS AN INTERIOR DESIGNER IN THE AIRCRAFT INDUSTRY.
SHE CURRENTLY WORKS AS A FREELANCE ILLUSTRATOR IN SÃO JOSÉ DOS
CAMPOS, BRAZIL. HER WORK HAS EXTENDED TO MANY DIFFERENT
APPLICATIONS, SUCH AS PET SUPPLIES, FOOD PACKAGING, STATIONERY,
AND FABRICS, AMONG OTHER PRODUCTS. HER CLIENTS INCLUDE PUBLIX,
CAMELOT FABRICS, NOTE CARD CAFE, BLUEBERRY PET, PICTURA USA,
FAB FIT FUN, AND FLOW MAGAZINE. MARINA LOVES BOOKS AND COFFEE,
THE PERFECT COMBINATION. SHE LIVES WITH HER HUSBAND, FRED, HER
SON, LORENZO, AND TWO CATS AND A DOG.

Library of Congress Cataloging-in-Publication data is available upon request.

ISBN: 978-1-955834-20-9

duopress books are available at special discounts when purchased in bulk for sales promotions as well as for fundraising or educational use. Special editions can be created to specification. Contact us at hello@duopressbooks.com for more information.

Manufactured in China
10 9 8 7 6 5 4 3 2 1

Duo Press, LLC.
8 Market Place, Suite 300
Baltimore, MD 21202

To order: hello@duopress.com

www.duopressbooks.com